THE GARDEN OF ENGLAND

painted by W. Biscombe Gardner

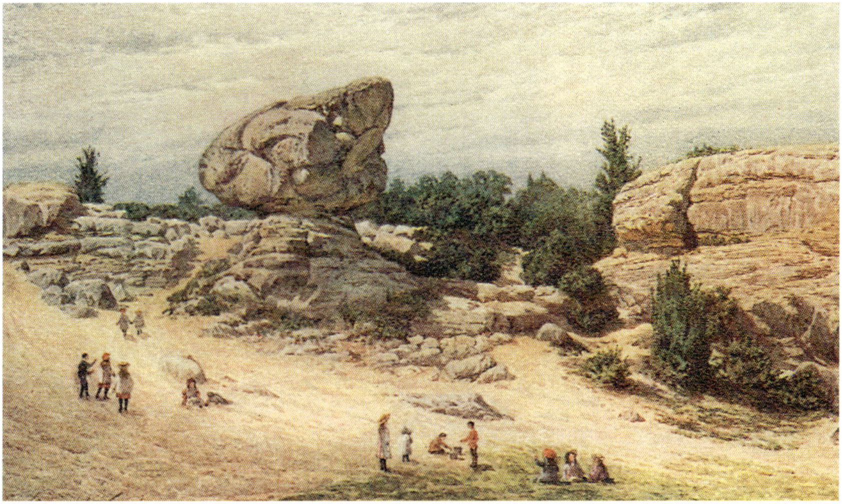

THE TOAD ROCK, TUNBRIDGE WELLS

SALMON

Published by
J Salmon Limited
100 London Road, Sevenoaks,
Kent TN13 1BB

First edition 1995

Designed by the Salmon Studio

ISBN 1 898435 27 8

Printed in England by
J Salmon Limited, Tubs Hill Works
Sevenoaks, Kent

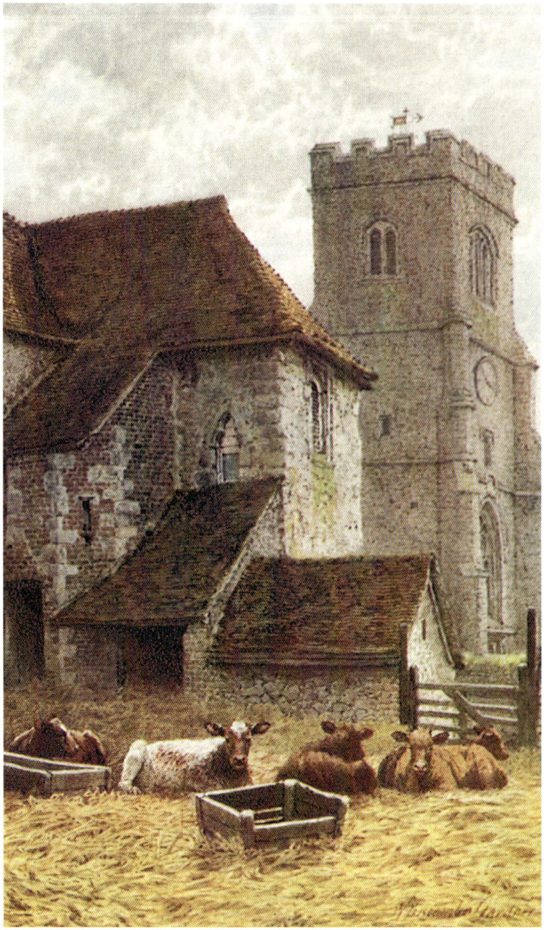

THE ARCHBISHOP'S PALACE AND CHURCH, CHARING

Coloured Illustrations

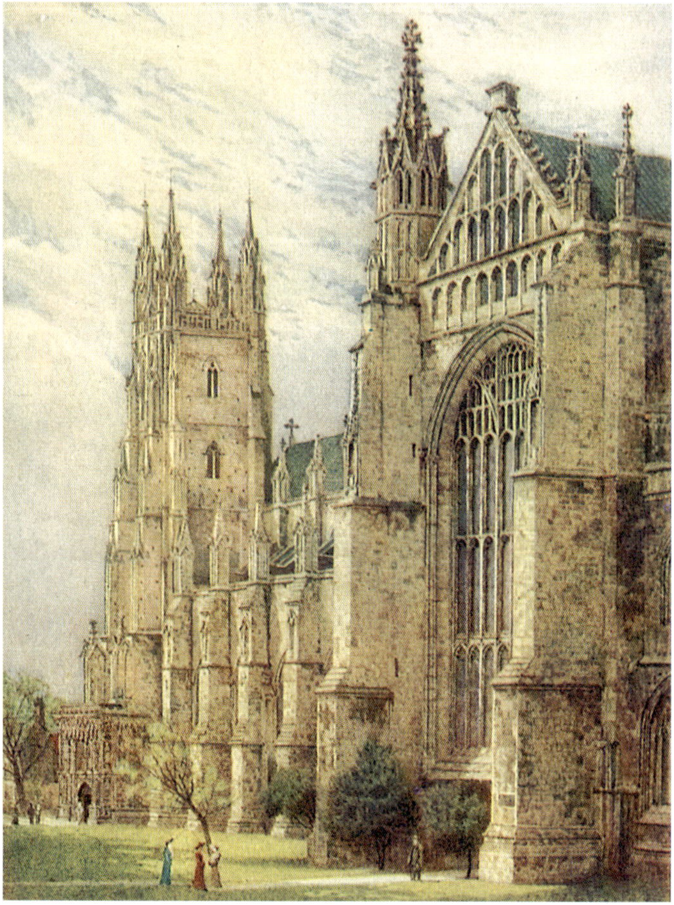

CANTERBURY CATHEDRAL, SOUTH SIDE

CANTERBURY

Were we to stand upon the summit of Bell Harry Tower of Canterbury Cathedral, looking down upon the city and countryside, much of the history of England would lie spread beneath our feet. The Britons were at work here before the Romans came marching with their legions; here to Ethelbert, Saxon king of Kent, St Augustine preached the gospel of Christ; in the church below, Becket was murdered and the Black Prince buried; to this city, to the shrine of St Thomas, came innumerable pilgrims, one of them Geoffrey Chaucer our first great English poet. Away to the east and south are the narrow seas, crossed by conquering Romans and Normans, to the north and west the Thames, Rochester and London. From no other tower, perhaps, can so wide a birds-eye view of our history be obtained.

It is to the cathedral that most first turn their steps, and rightly so. Entering the close by Christchurch Gateway, completed in 1517, one looks up at Bell Harry, centre of the cathedral as the cathedral is of the city. As one passes round, by the ruins of the Infirmary and the Dark Entry, and enters the grandeur of the interior, it is at once apparent that Canterbury is a growth of long ages, the handiwork of many generations of builders.

Canterbury is still in many ways a medieval city. We can enter it by the 14th century West Gate, the one gateway mercifully spared out of six and walk down an old-world high street, overlooked by gabled houses. We can stop awhile on the King's Bridge to admire the old home of the Canterbury Weavers, the sluggish waters of the many-branched Stour flowing beneath. We can chance upon the Grey Friars, standing on arches above the waters of the river and appreciate that Canterbury is a place of churches, of priories, and of monasteries.

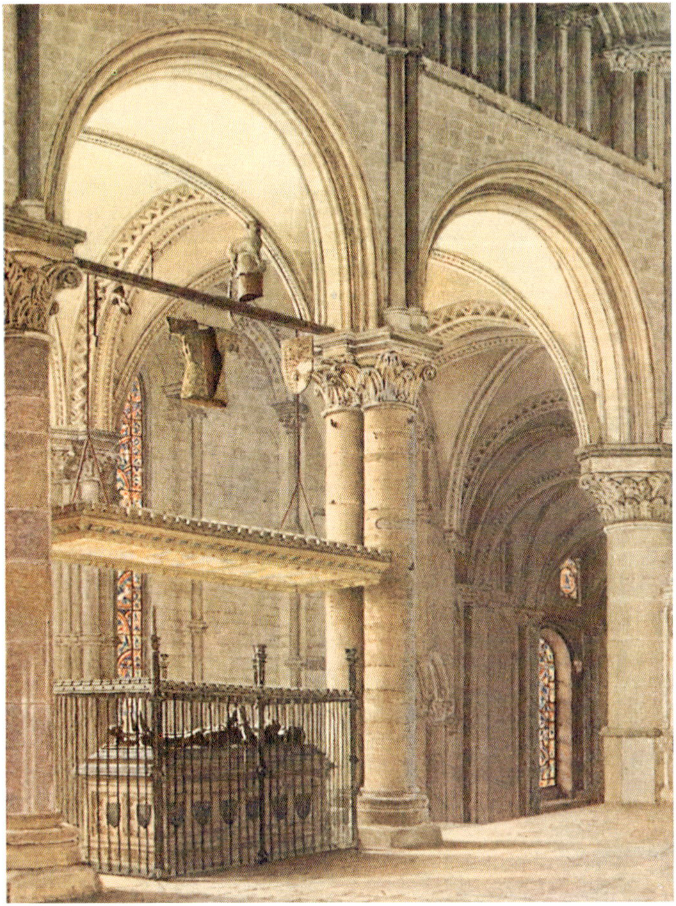

THE BLACK PRINCE'S TOMB, CANTERBURY CATHEDRAL

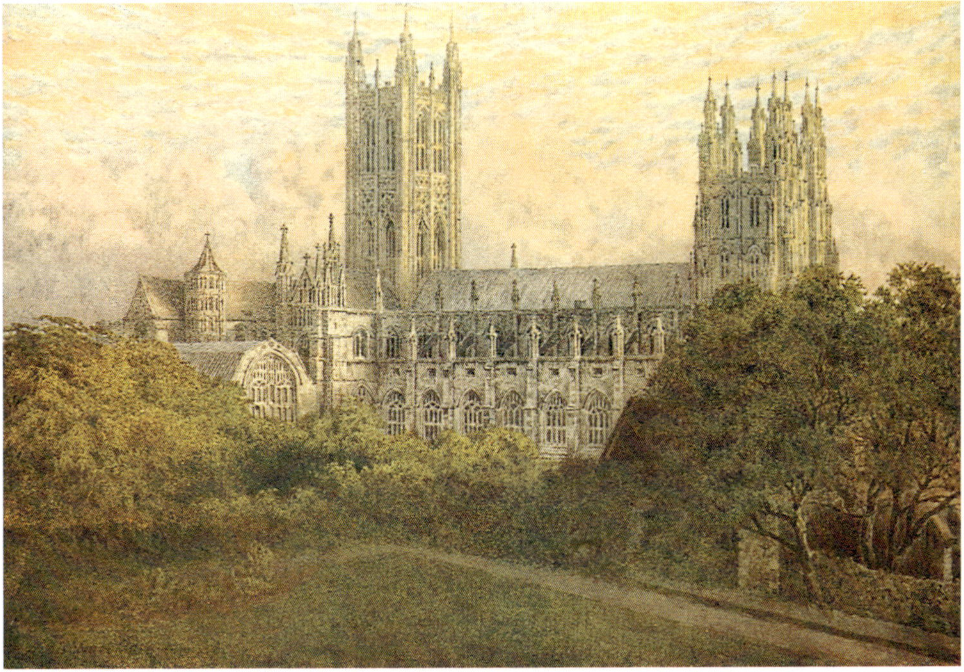

CANTERBURY CATHEDRAL

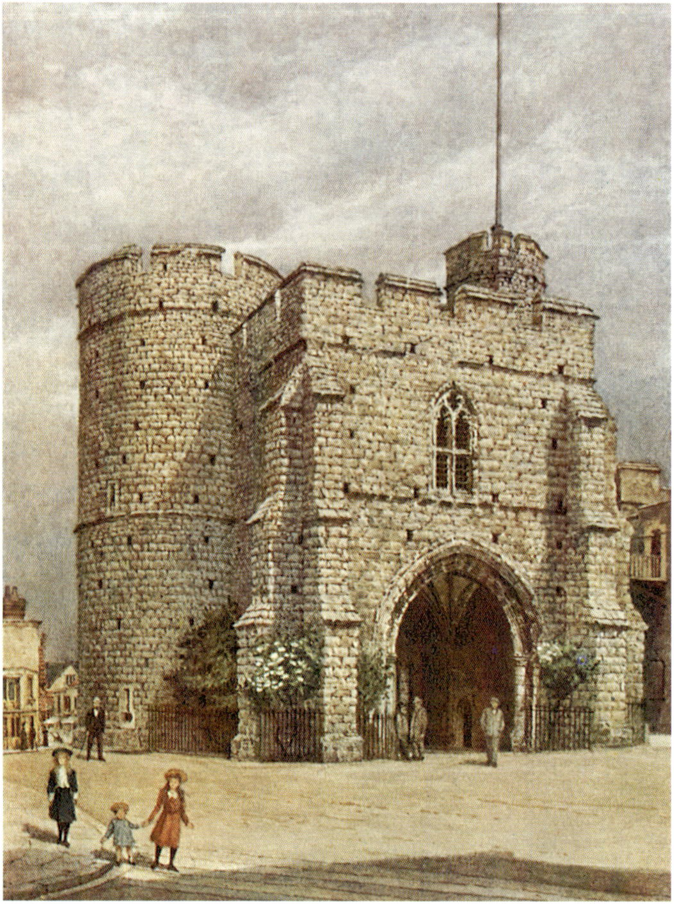

THE WESTGATE, CANTERBURY

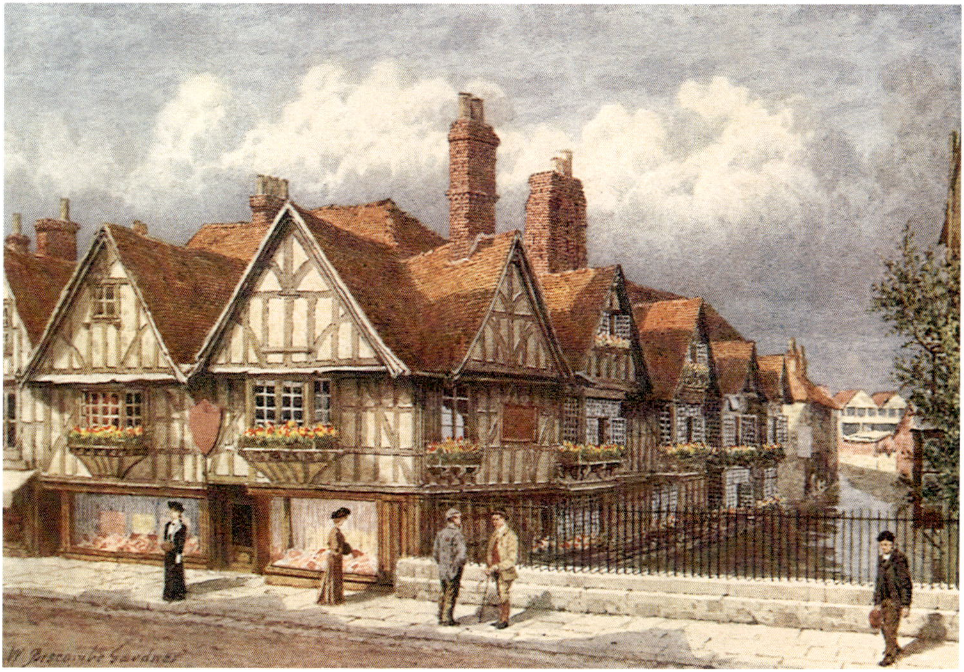

THE WEAVERS, CANTERBURY

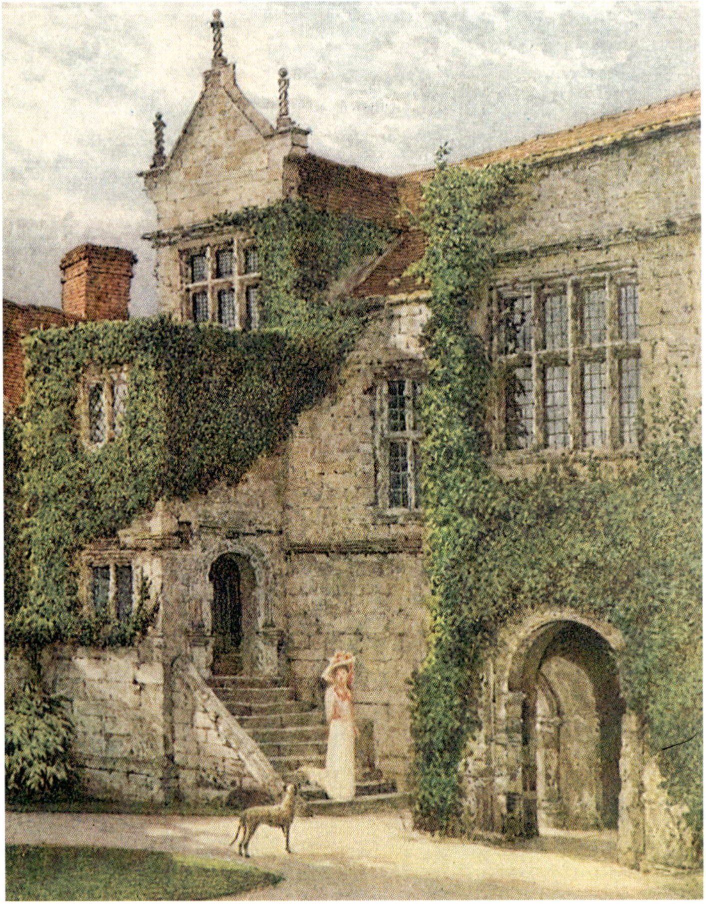

THE ARCHBISHOP'S PALACE, MAIDSTONE

AROUND MAIDSTONE

and the River Medway

To most men the Medway, if known at all, stands for a broad arm of the sea that reaches up inland to Chatham and Rochester, beyond which it is but a name. Yet to those who love country streams this river is full of charm and interest. No castled crags frown down upon its placid waters but there are castles on its banks; it flows serenely past green hills and pleasant pastures, dividing the land of the Kentish Men from that of the Men of Kent.

To stand upon the grassy heights of the North Downs above Birling is to appreciate the magnificent breadth of this part of Kent. Away to the north the Medway, broadening out, passes under Rochester Bridge, with its attendant castle and cathedral and echoes of Charles Dickens; opposite range wood-clad hills, breaking up into well tilled fields and there, running along the gentle decline, is the narrow thread of the Pilgrims' Way; to the east is Maidstone, dimly visible, and, as one turns southward, a blurred glory of woods and hills, church spires and tall houses, broad fields and meadows and strips of white road.

Maidstone, the capital of Kent, lies for the most part on the right bank of the Medway, and an old county-town atmosphere pervades it. The Church of All Saints, pleasantly situated above the river, is handsome; around it are the College and the Archbishop's Palace. The three edifices group harmoniously, forming a pleasant prospect from the other side of the river. Maidstone is the centre of hop-country, a landscape of churches and castles, of parks and village greens – a country to be visited at any time of year with delight. Around and about are many interesting places; Aylesford with its red-roofed houses and picturesque Friary, Allington Castle, grim in its riverside setting, West Malling, with its wide main street and striking Norman Abbey.

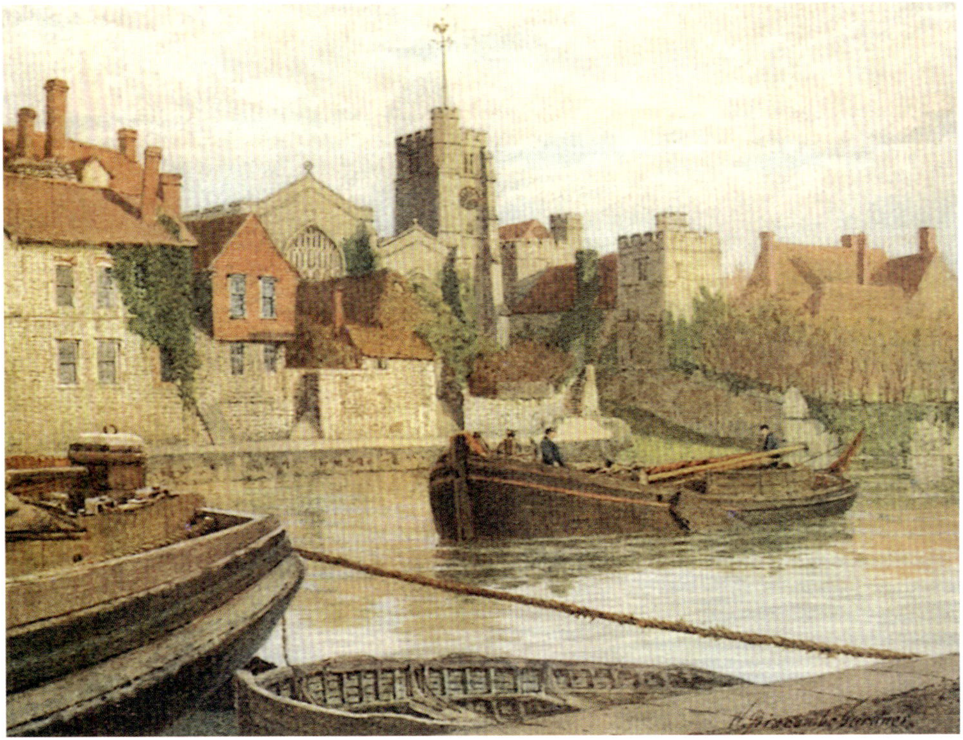

THE RIVER MEDWAY AT MAIDSTONE

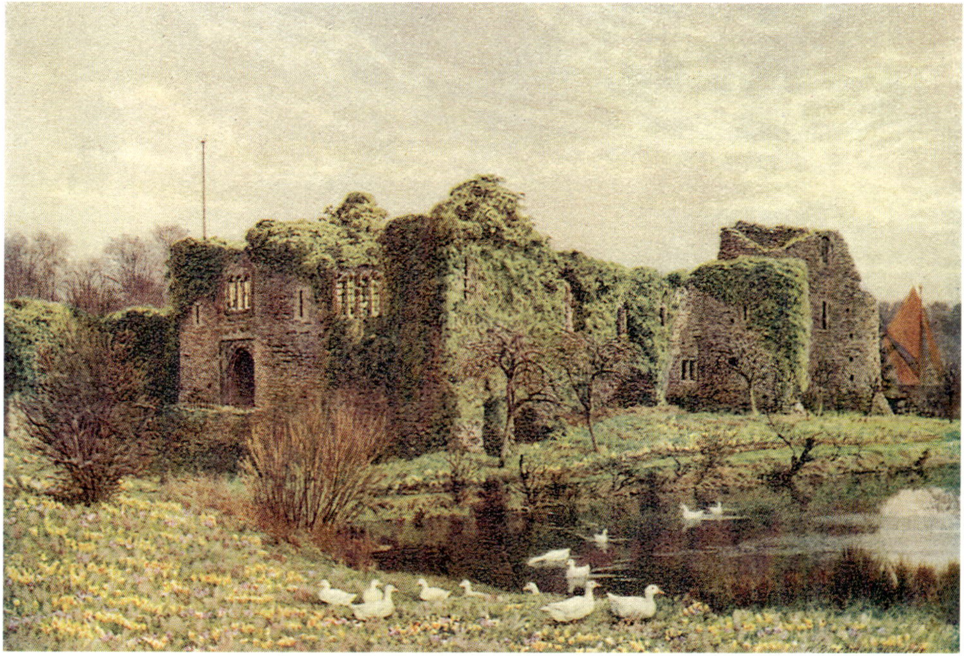

ALLINGTON CASTLE

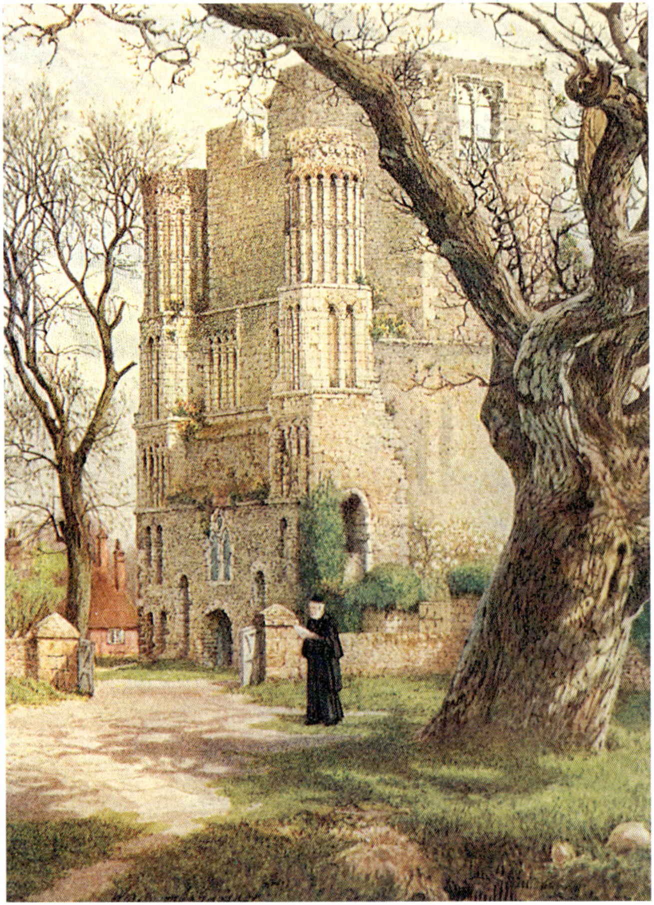

ST. LEONARD'S TOWER, MALLING ABBEY

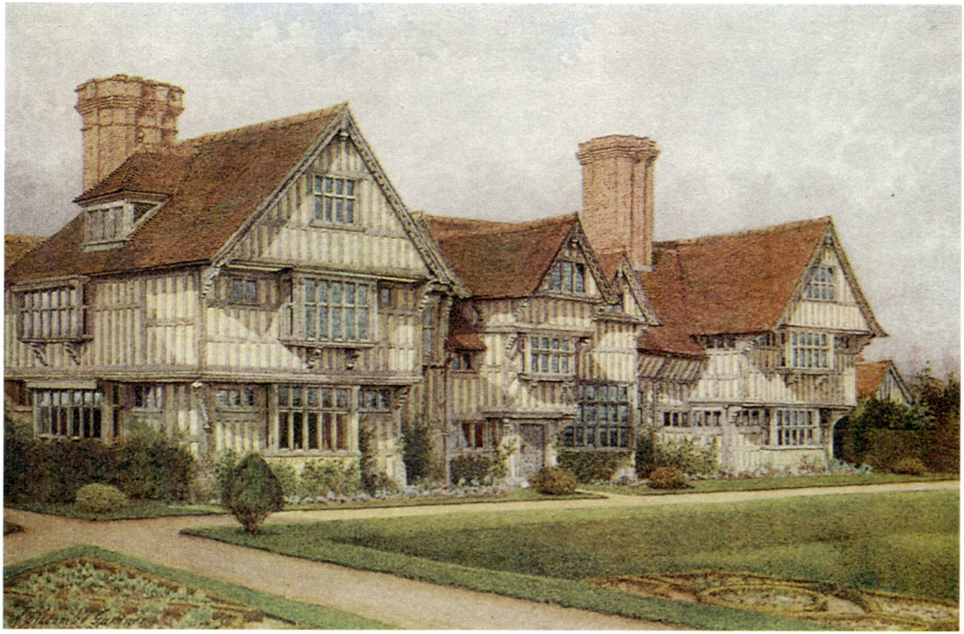

RUMWOOD COURT, LANGLEY

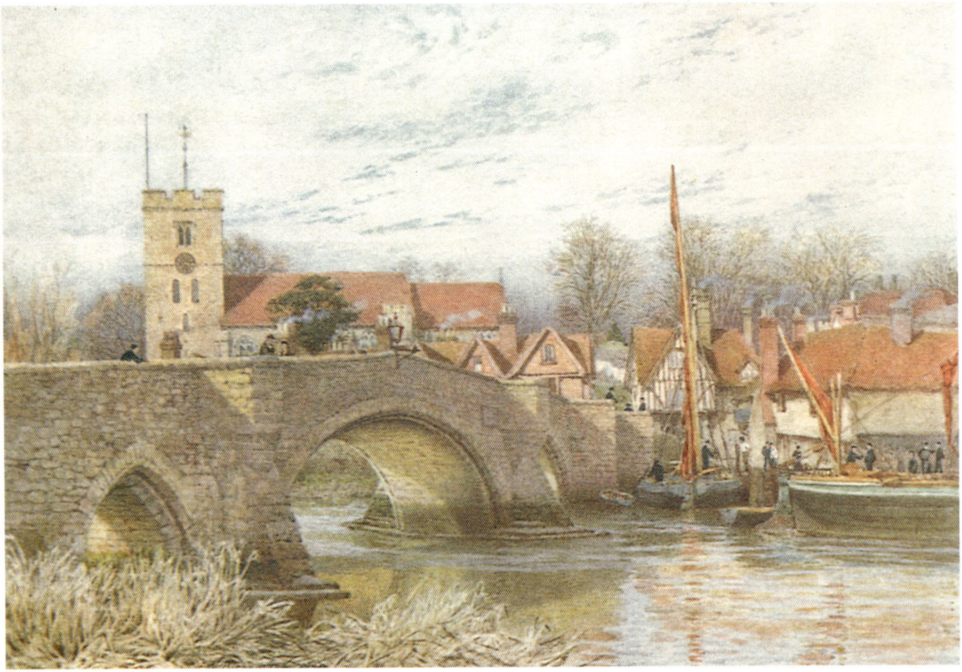

AYLESFORD BRIDGE, RIVER MEDWAY

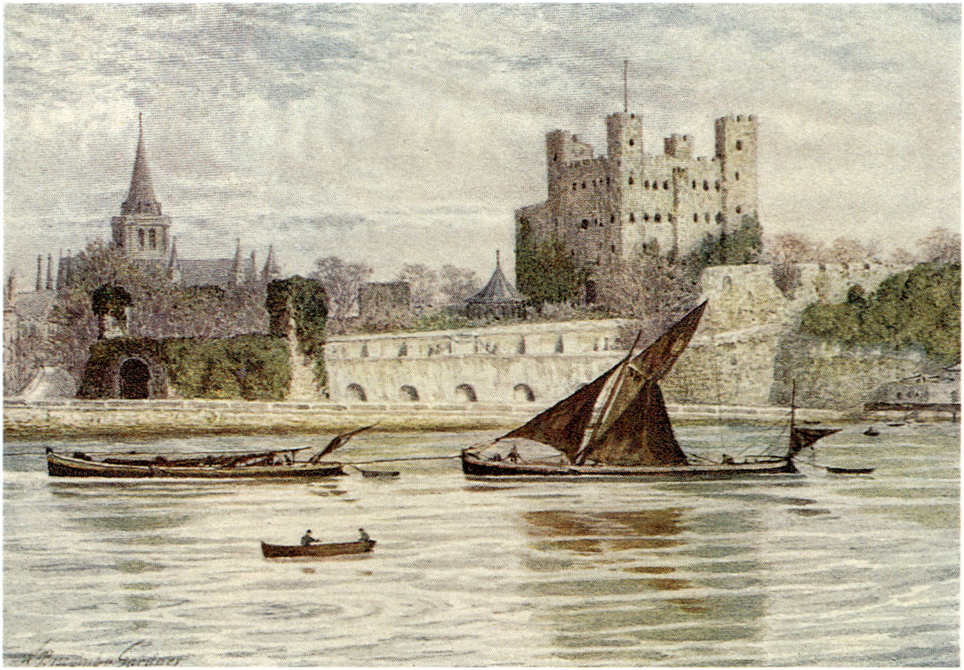

ROCHESTER CATHEDRAL AND CASTLE

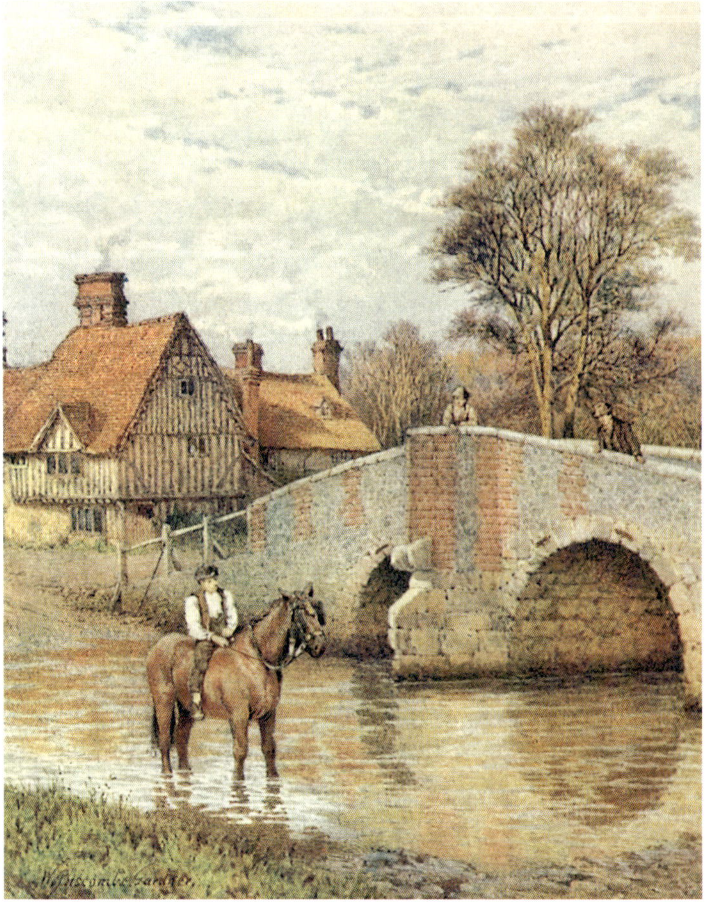

EYNSFORD BRIDGE AND FORD

WEST KENT

In the western corner of Kent there lives still a country of foaming orchards, of primrose and bluebell woods, of sedate villages, and of little surprises waiting to be discovered around each corner. True you may perhaps find a deeper rusticity in certain parts of Suffolk or Norfolk, or in the heart of Wessex, but the garden country of Kent has its own special appeal – the North Downs make an effective barrier between its villages and towns and the spread of London.

A perfect example of a little country town is Wolfe's birthplace, Westerham, which lies beside the slender Darent. On the slope of the nearby North Downs you may still walk, untroubled by your fellows, part of the old track of the Pilgrims' Way, or you can follow the course of the infant river downstream, stopping awhile in the villages of Otford, Shoreham and Eynsford, nestling in the valley bottom beside the clear rushing waters. Or you may go south by the little bridge across the stream and mount to Brasted Chart. From the sandy paths, at a height of 800 feet, you may look for miles across the real Kentish country, merging eastward into the blue Weald and southward to the darker line of the South Downs. The ridge, clad in gorse and heather and woodland, runs for several miles on either hand, and the view is good all the way along the winding lanes which skirt it, and which, here and there, reveal a cluster of typical Kentish cottages, with red, deep-dipping roofs.

From Toys Hill a road through pleasant, pastoral countryside goes down to Chiddingstone and Penshurst; Chiddingstone with its line of old timbered houses, its inn beside the castle gates, and noble church, sleeping among the quiet meadows that surround it. From here it is but two miles on foot to lovely Penshurst, and a few more miles to ancient Tonbridge, and to Royal Tunbridge Wells, with its fine air and breezy commons, its historic associations and the countryside at its door.

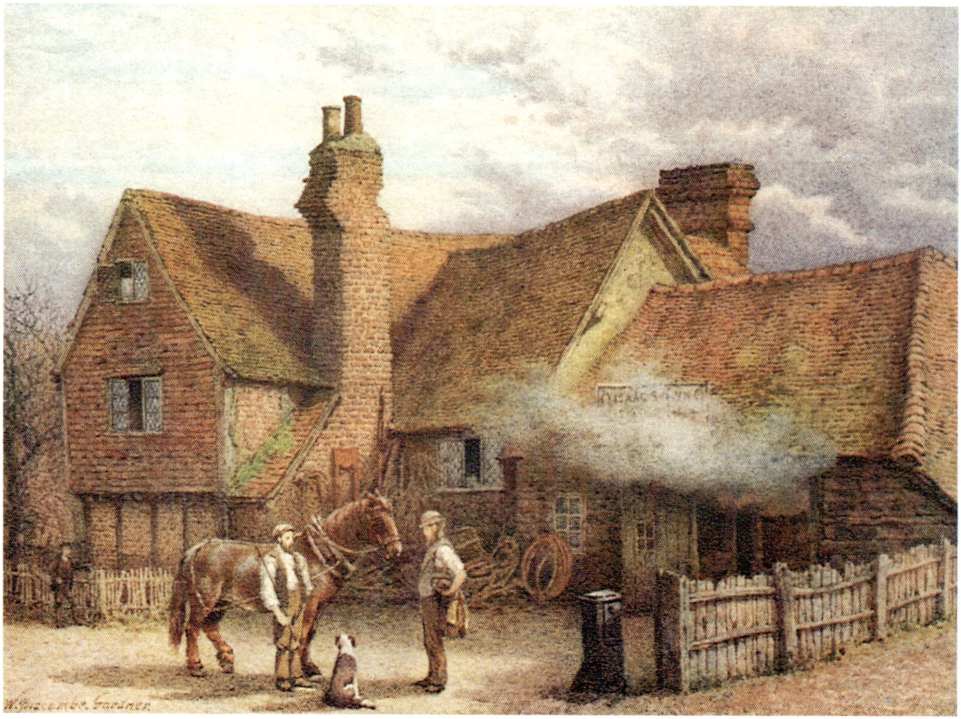

THE OLD SMITHY, SHOREHAM

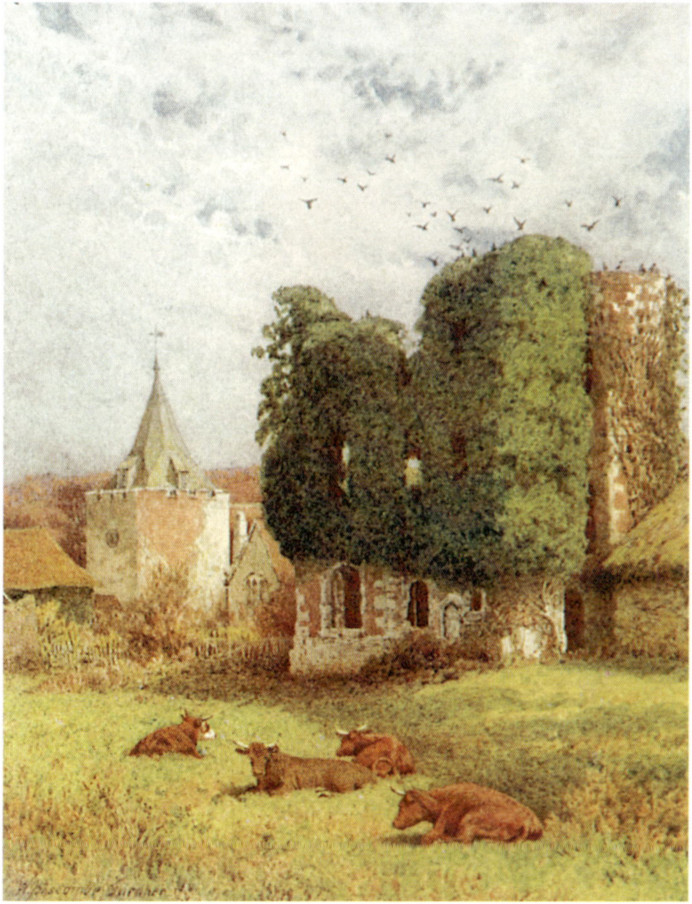

OTFORD CASTLE AND CHURCH

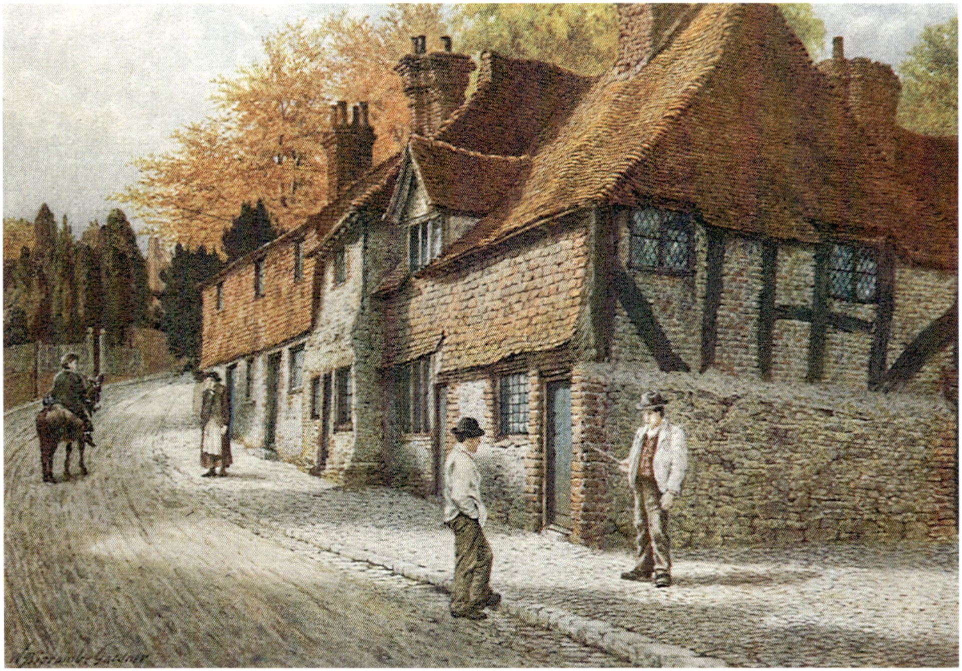

THE OLD ALMSHOUSES, WESTERHAM

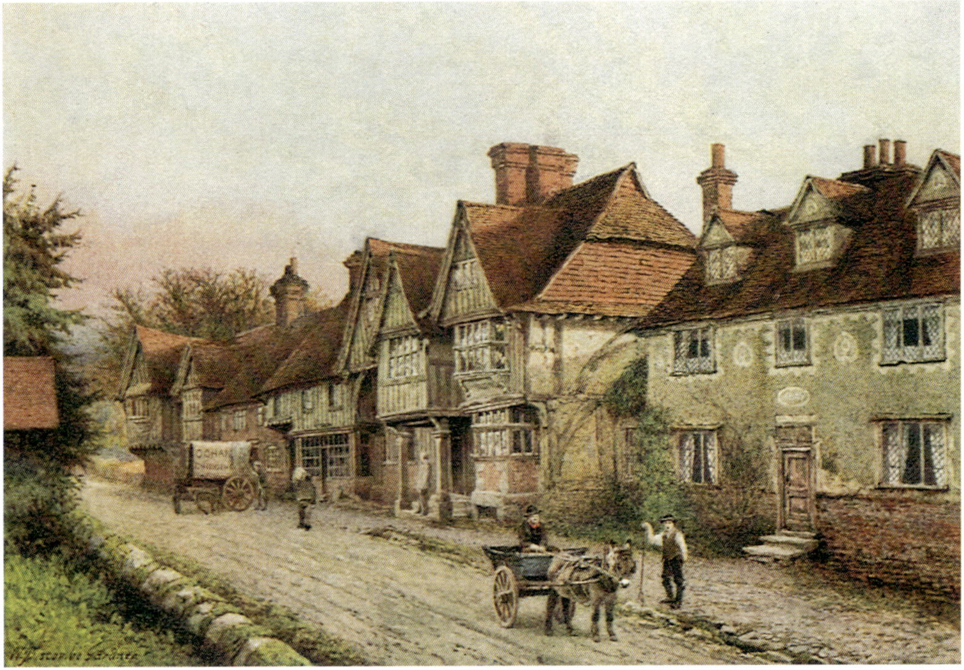

CHIDDINGSTONE

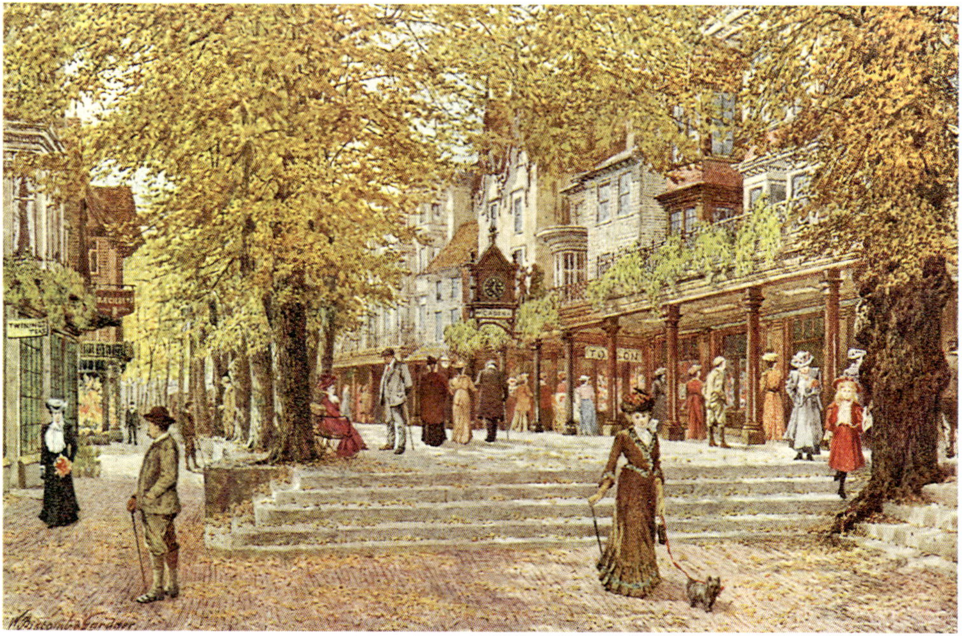

THE PANTILES, TUNBRIDGE WELLS

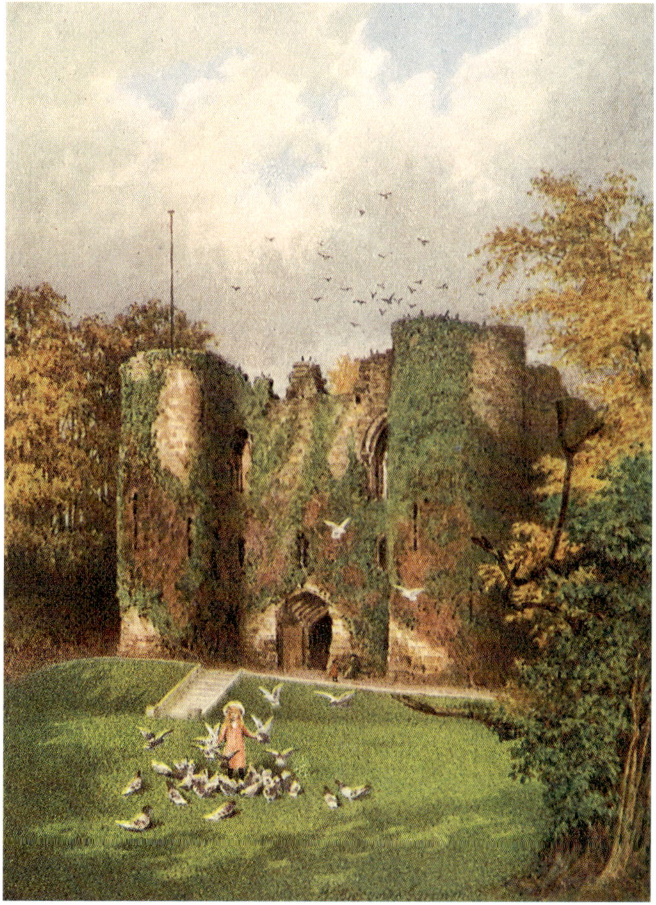

TONBRIDGE CASTLE

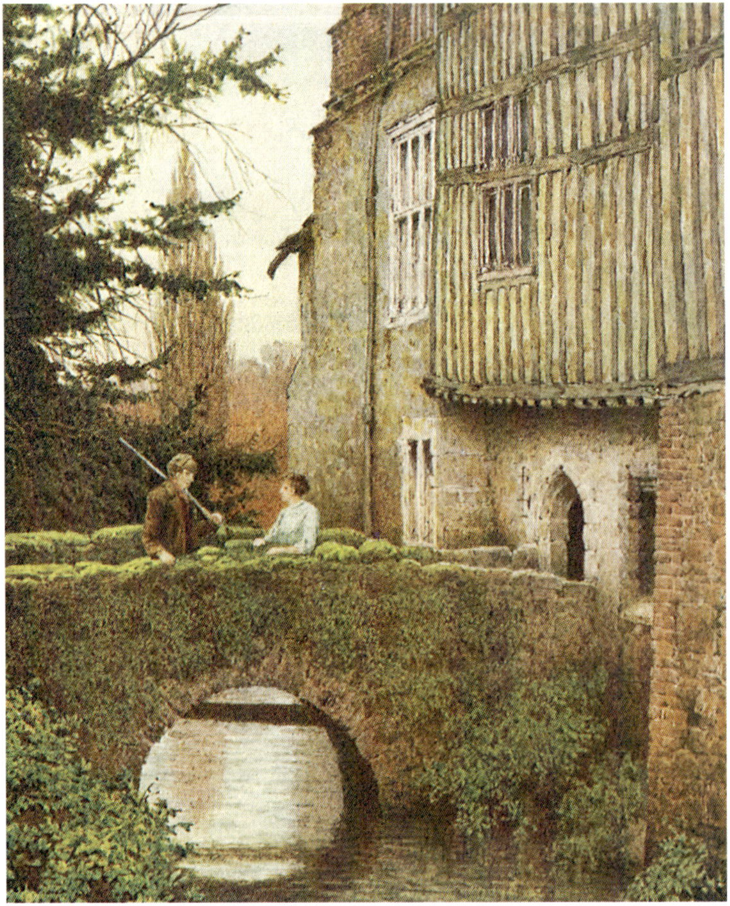

THE EAST BRIDGE, IGHTHAM MOTE

SOME NOBLE HOUSES

Kent is the county of comfortable homes – Knole, Penshurst, Hever and Ightham and many another, big and small, each with its individual air but all bearing that harmony with the the landscape which only the passage of the centuries can bestow.

It is best to approach Penshurst from the north, for almost immediately the house comes into view under the outstretched arms of a stalwart oak. As one walks around and through the grounds the charm of the building and the gardens lays hold upon the heart; the trimly clipped yew hedges, the splendid blaze of the roses, the fruit trees with their tones of russet and green, the view over the lush valley of the Medway, and, centre of all this loveliness and commanding it, Penshurst Place itself, with high-peaked roofs, tall turrets, and quaint chimney stacks. A grassy path leads round the house and its lawns to a gateway into the churchyard with its attendant lych-gate.

Hever Castle is but some two miles distant from Penshurst, surrounded by its moat, fed from the River Eden; a quadrangle of gabled buildings, around which lingers an air of romance, the love story of Henry VIII and Anne Boleyn. Not far away, embraced by its rolling deer park, is another noble home; Knole is a giant of a house, with its 365 rooms, built of the grey Kentish rag and covered with deep-toned red tiles. As we wander through the halls and corridors we mingle with the living past – we meet kings and queens, soldiers and statesmen, courtiers and great ladies.

Then there is idyllic Ightham Mote, one of the few remaining specimens of a moated manor house, its walls rising sheer from the still waters. Of a totally different character – a fortress and a home – is Leeds Castle; as at Ightham there is a moat but here it is a broad lake from which springs the stately stronghold.

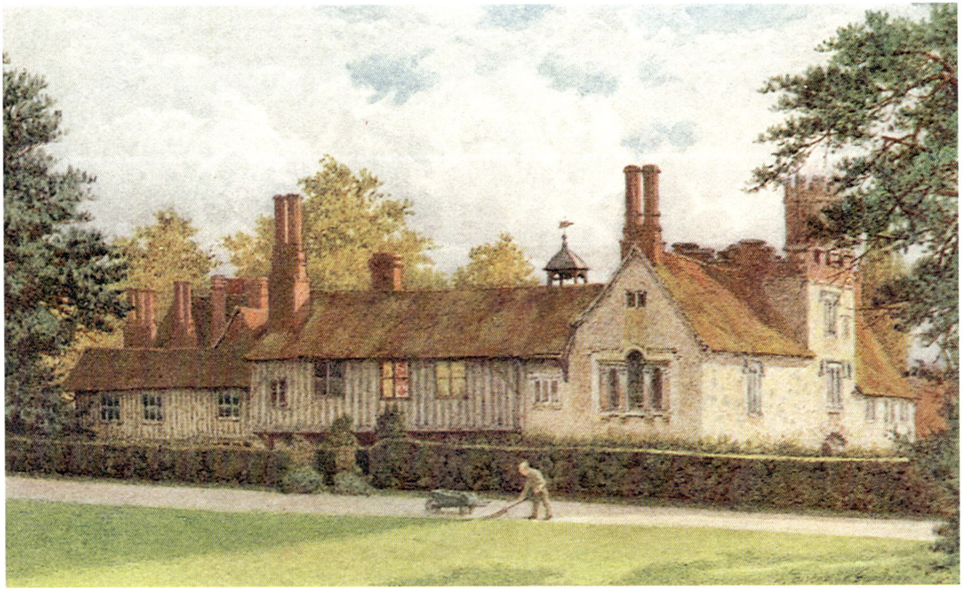

IGHTHAM MOTE FROM THE BOWLING GREEN

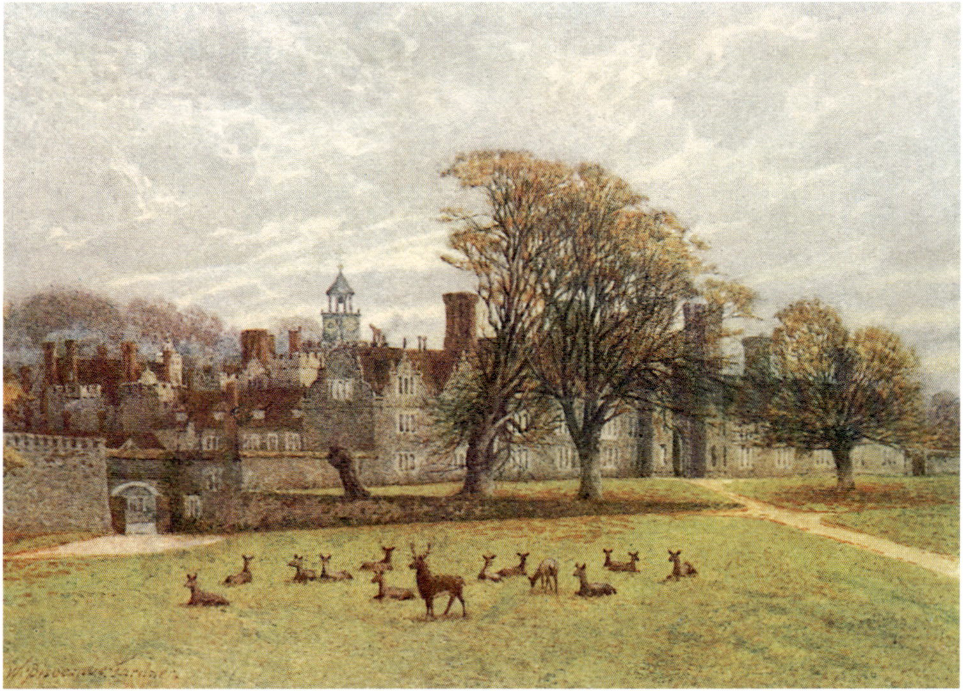

KNOLE FROM THE PARK

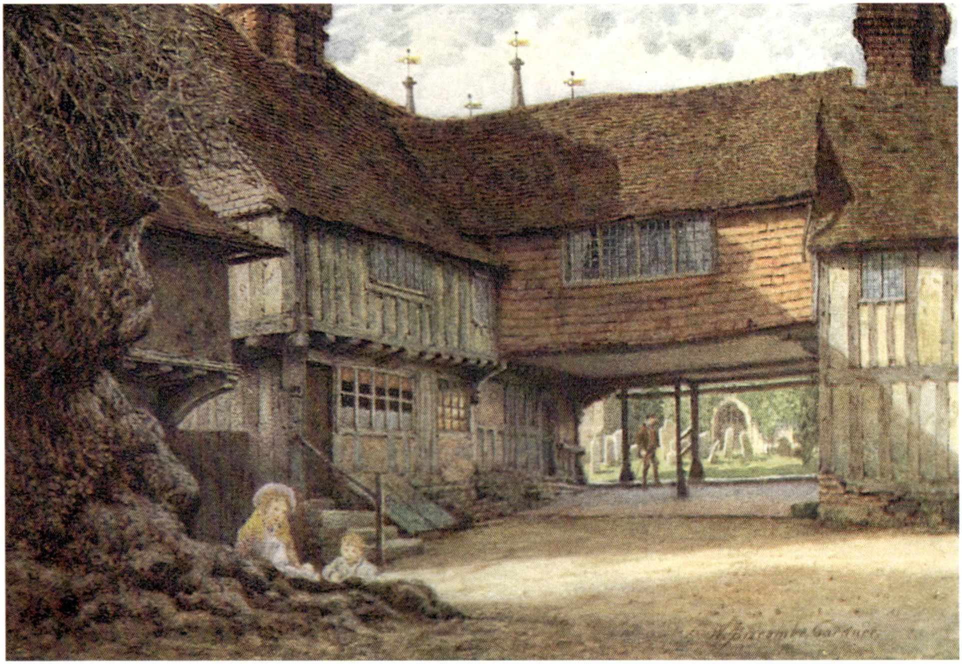

LEICESTER SQUARE, PENSHURST

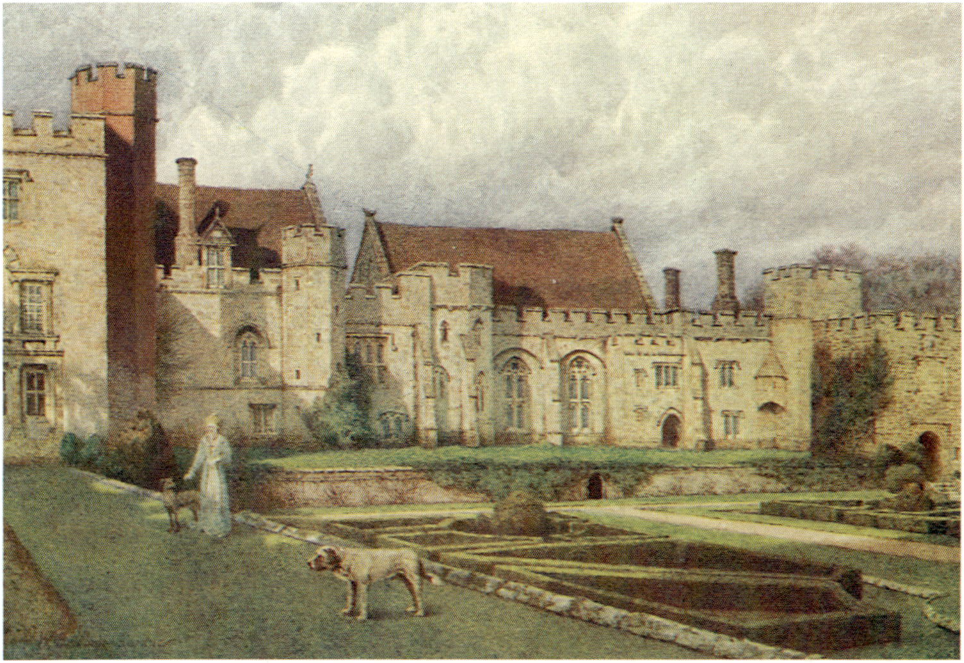

PENSHURST PLACE FROM THE TERRACE

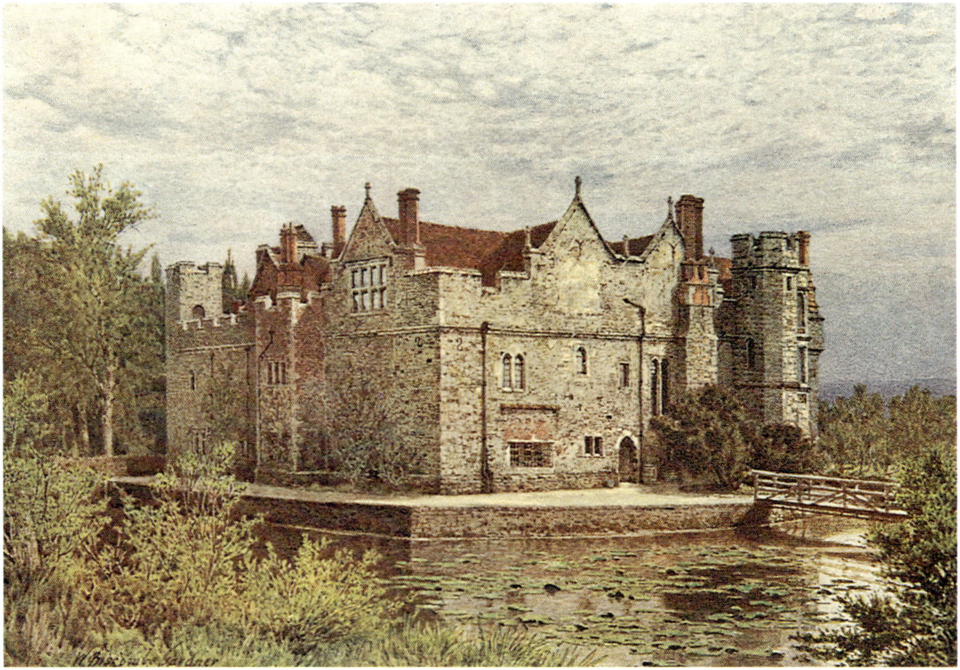

HEVER CASTLE

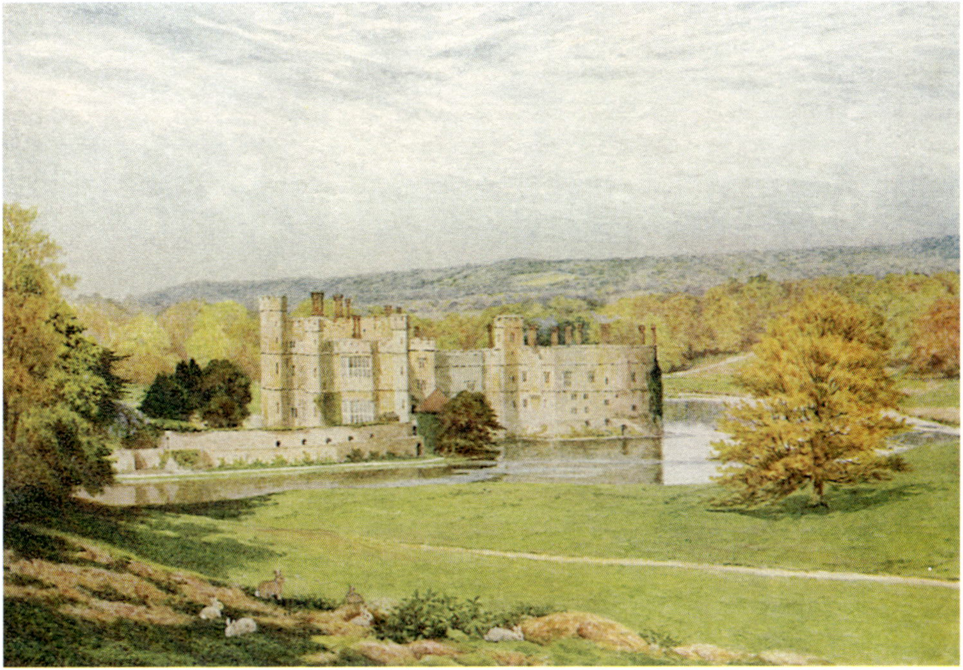

SPRINGTIME AT LEEDS CASTLE

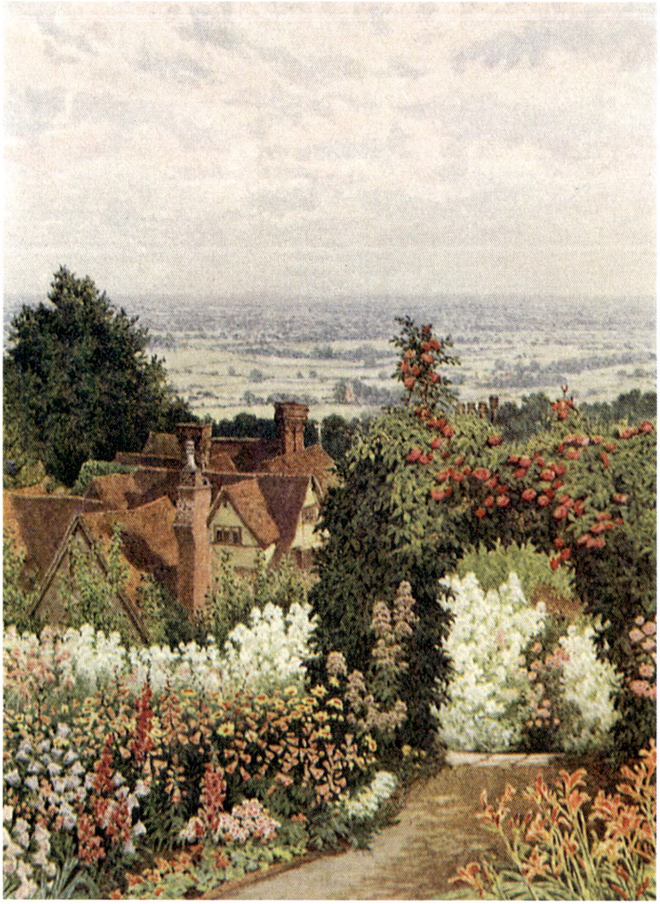

THE WEALD FROM SUTTON VALENCE

THE WEALD

Perhaps the very best of Kent lies in the Weald country of hop-gardens and oast houses and spinneys and pastures, and the best of the villages, or small towns, in that group which cluster around Biddenden and Cranbrook, Goudhurst and Brenchley, Tenterden and Hawkhurst. To look down in summertime into the Weald from the tops of the adjacent hills is to enjoy the finest prospect possible, the whole view being composed of cornfields and meadows of different colours adorned with all manner of flowers, of green woods and hedgerows, and of towns and villages, here and there interspersed.

One does not tire easily of the appeal of the Weald. It is as good to follow its winding lanes in December as in May, for leafless spinneys and stubble fields and the lines of an harmonious landscape have a separate beauty under winter skies. The sharp smell of newly turned earth is as sweet then as the softer fragrances of spring, when the larks and robins and finches flutter from field and hedgerow. Nothing about this countryside can be named as a feature, but it is deeply English, and through even the longest acquaintance it continues to satisfy.

There is nothing more pleasant or delightful on a spring or summer's day than to follow the country road that meanders through Brenchley and Horsmonden, past Goudhurst in its hilltop setting and the red-brick tower of Sissinghurst Castle, and on, by the stone-flagged paths of Biddenden, to Tenterden, the jewel of the Weald and set unchangeable in dignity. It is a quiet centre from which to explore Romney Marsh and the Isle of Oxney, and the trees and grass which line each side of its street, the soaring church and the Tudor shops and houses, create a scene which compels the stranger passing through it to pause.

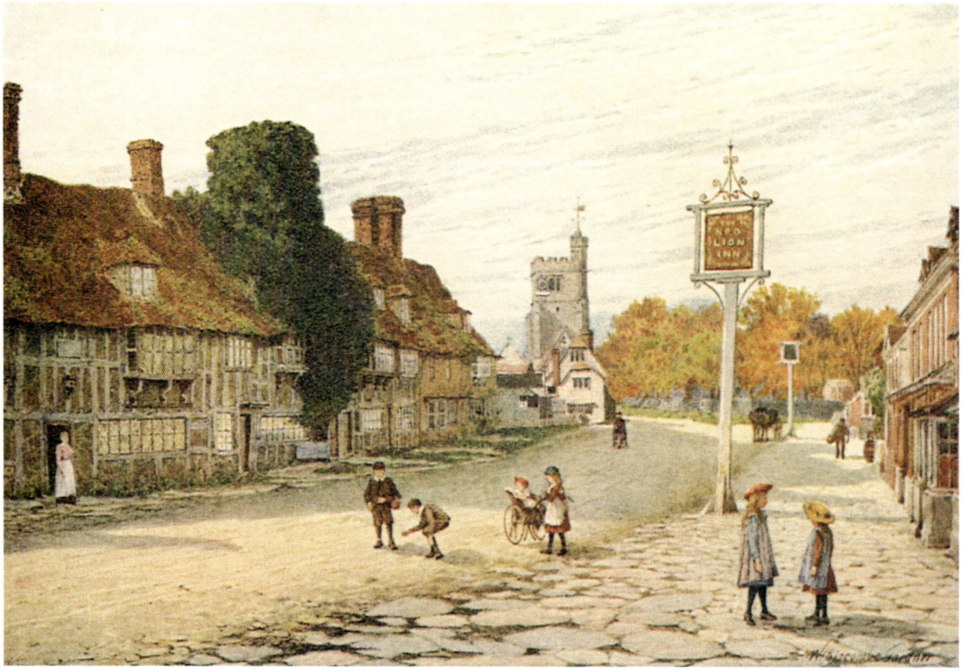

BIDDENDEN

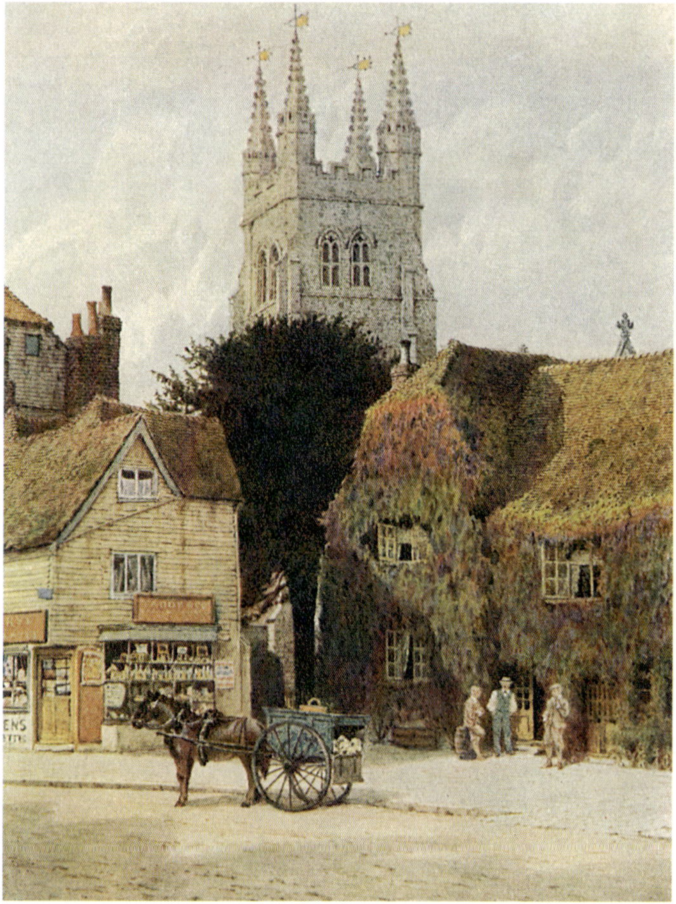

THE CHURCH AND 'WOOLPACK', TENTERDEN

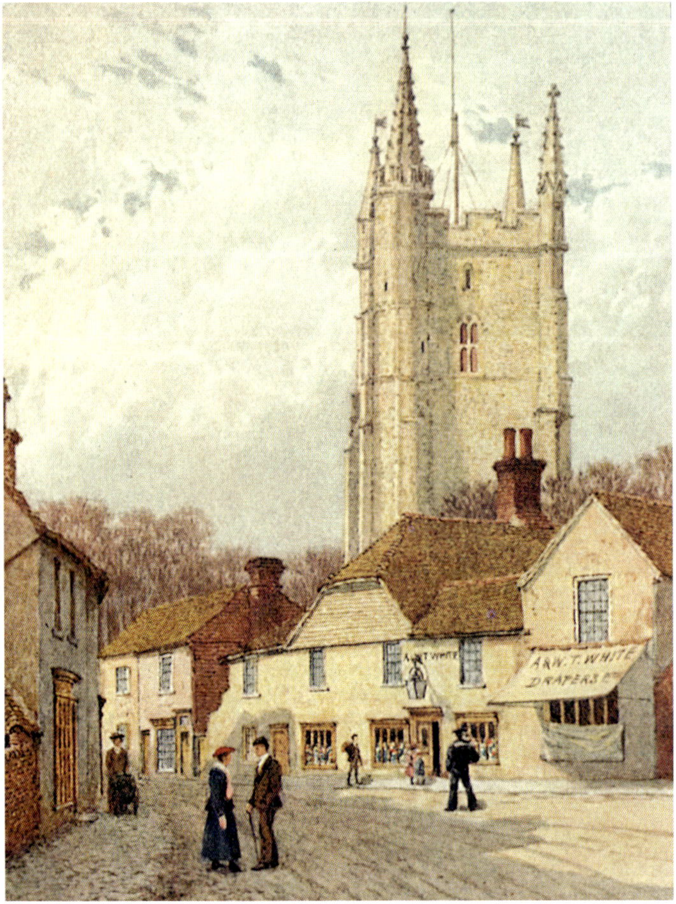

CORONATION SQUARE, LYDD

ROMNEY MARSH

Three miles to the south of Tenterden, on the edge of the Isle of Oxney, is Smallhythe, the landing stage for the town when it was something of a little port on the Rother estuary; today it comprises only of a church and two half-timbered cottages. But here you are close upon the Marsh and upon haunted land. It is not that ghosts will meet you on the innumerable twists by narrow and lonely lanes to Ham Street, or by Appledore on its little hill, or by Brenzett to Romney and Lydd. But along those reedy streams, beloved of the heron and the wild duck, across those empty fields, and by the very walls of the old farmhouses, you will be aware of a presence that defies definition and whose power can only be called the Spirit of the Marsh.

In summer the air shimmers with a brighter light above the sprouting corn than in more inhabited country, and the sculptured clouds seem to be visitants from another world. In winter the frost-bound silence has a voice, for the Marsh never sleeps in any hour or season, but conveys always that sense of vital but invisible life which is everywhere about us, but which, where men are gathered in communities, is obscured and muted. You hate the Marsh or you love it and for those captured by its embrace it will hold as powerfully as the Fens hold their lovers.

If you follow the broad curves of the Royal Military Canal, through the charm of the valley pastures by which this waterway passes to the sea at Hythe, you will get a feeling for the landscape of this Kentish corner. Southward stretches the Marsh, pastel-toned under the wind or hazy with heat; northward a line of wooded hills, sheltering comfortable farms and grazing lands. A superb view may be had from a bluff of these hills at Lympne, a faintly etched picture of marsh and sea and sky, so subtly arranged that the flat lands below seem locked eternally in the embrace of the water.

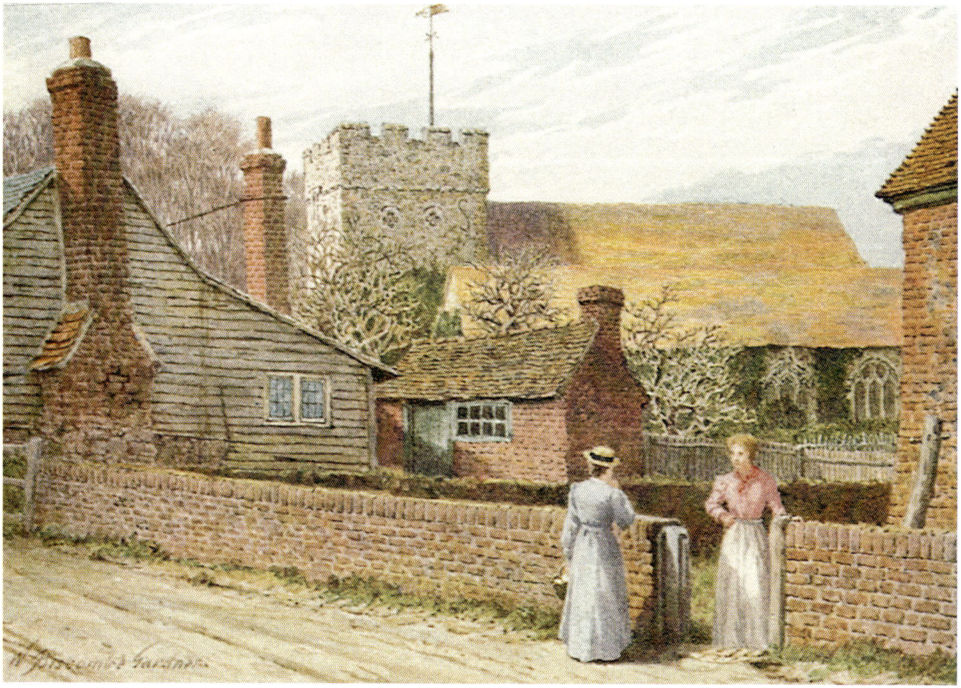

AN OLD CORNER, APPLEDORE

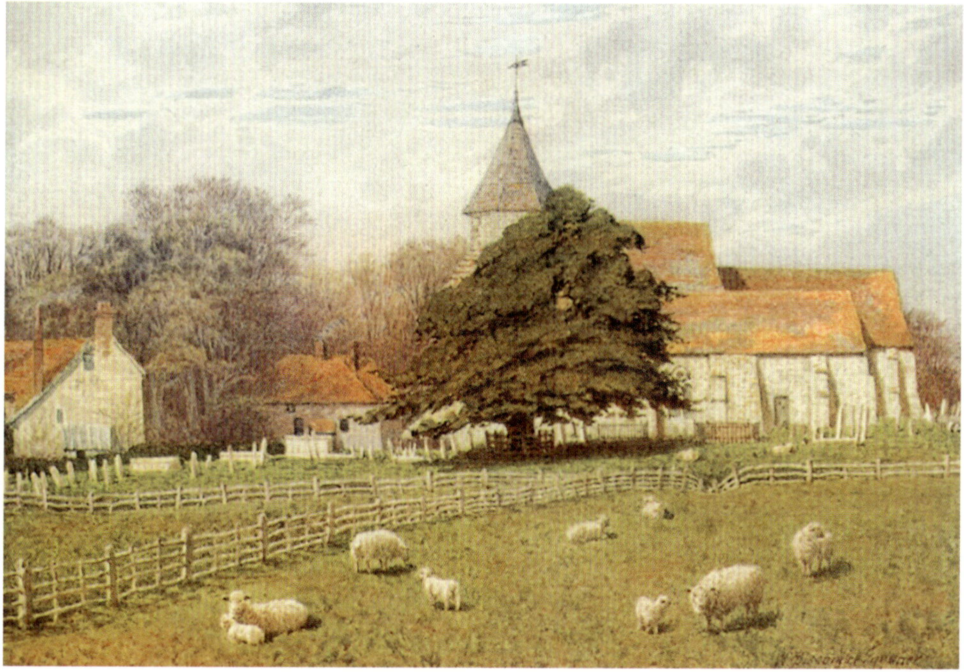

THE CHURCH, OLD ROMNEY

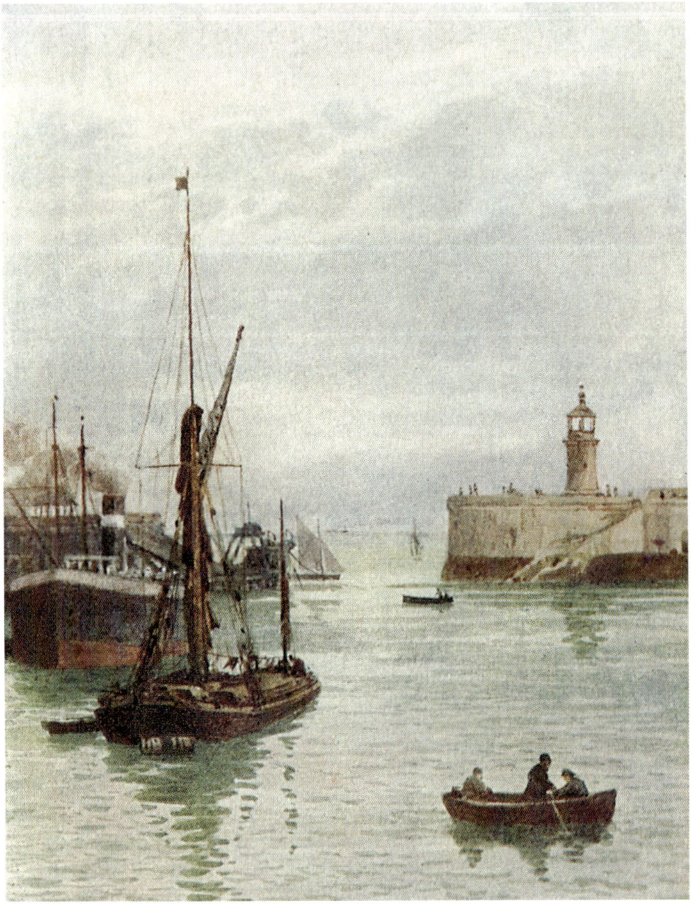

IN RAMSGATE HARBOUR

THE KENT COAST

History and natural beauty have allied to lend interest and enchantment to the shores that lie between the Reculvers and Dover. Whilst there are other parts of our coasts more grand, around none can one trace with more delight the passage of great men and the relics of past days, nor where the story of the sea is more redolent of adventure and achievement. Kent has ever been the outpost of England. Men have crossed and recrossed the narrow seas that divide Britain from France; in Kent landed Caesar, the Saxons and St Augustine. As we walk along the summit of the white cliffs the air is filled with echoes of the past.

As one stands on the beach at Herne Bay, some few miles off the twin towers of Reculver Church silhouette against the sky; now close to the waves, but once some considerable distance therefrom. Beyond is bustling Margate, and, over the springy turf of the North Foreland, where a beacon has stood for centuries to warn mariners off the treacherous Goodwin Sands, Broadstairs, with its atmosphere of Dickens. Southwards lie the Cinque Ports of Ramsgate and Sandwich, 'the village on the sands', a picturesque relic of glorious days when the sea came up to its quays. Inland is Minster, a charming village embowered in trees on the verge of the marshes.

At Deal the houses of the old town seem, as it were, to be anxious to take a dip in the sea, but when Henry VIII set up the castles of Walmer and Deal there was considerable space of land before the waves. Not so at Dover, whose white cliffs have long been the bulwark of England; from no vantage point does its Norman castle look so strong and imposing as from the sea. And so to Folkestone, a pleasant watering place with its old town and harbour, where stairs and zig-zag paths lead down between the cliffs and the sea.

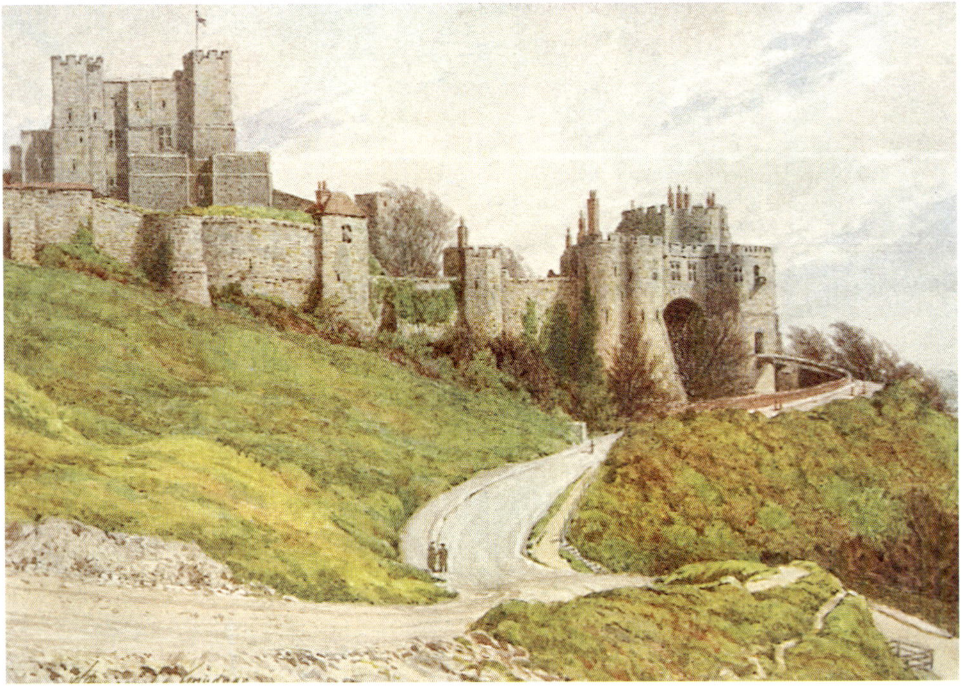

DOVER CASTLE

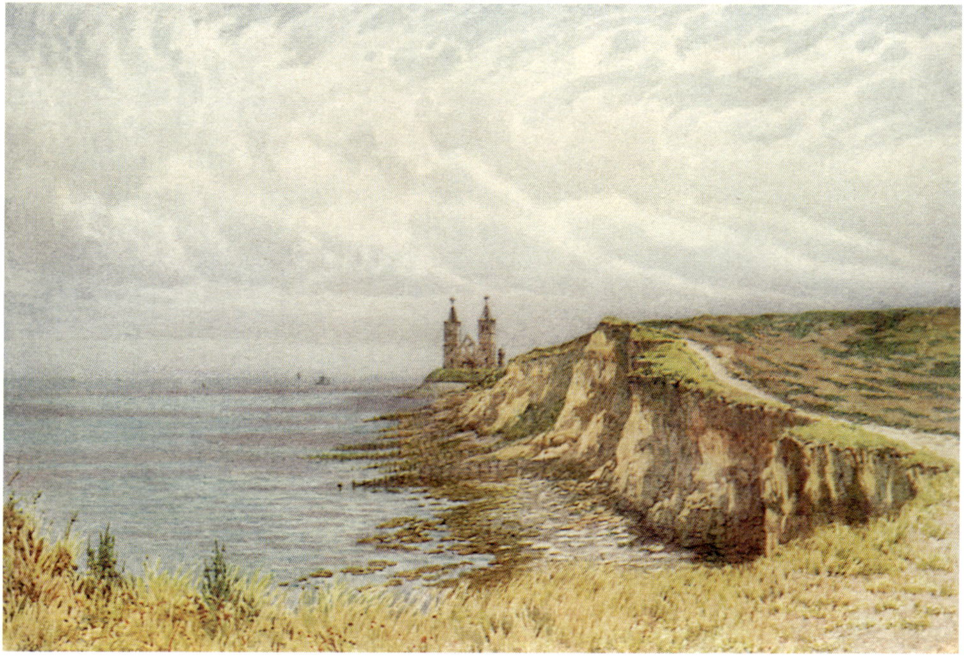

RECULVER FROM THE WEST

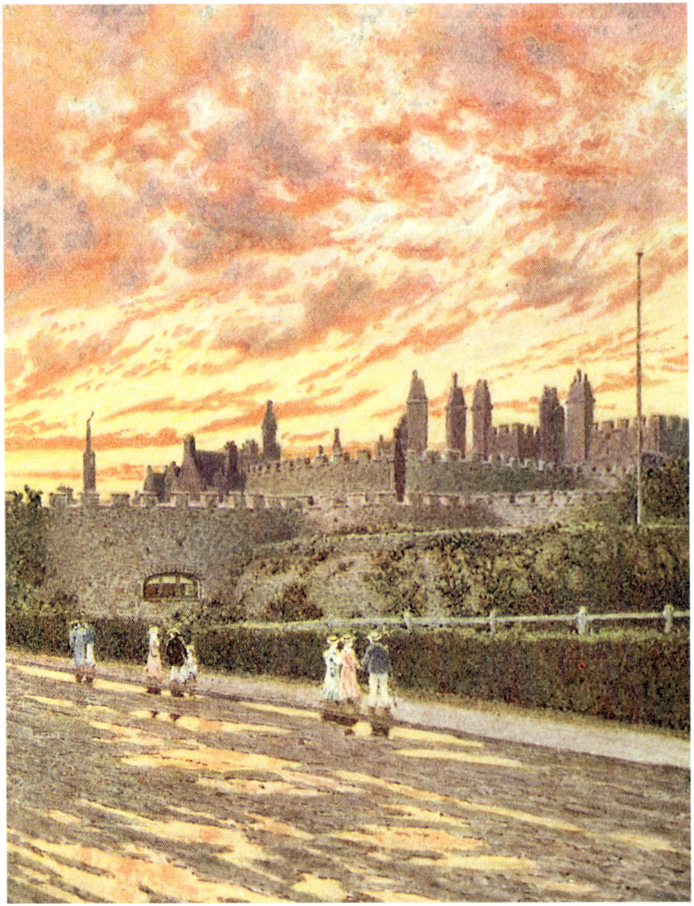

DEAL CASTLE – CLOSE OF A STORMY DAY

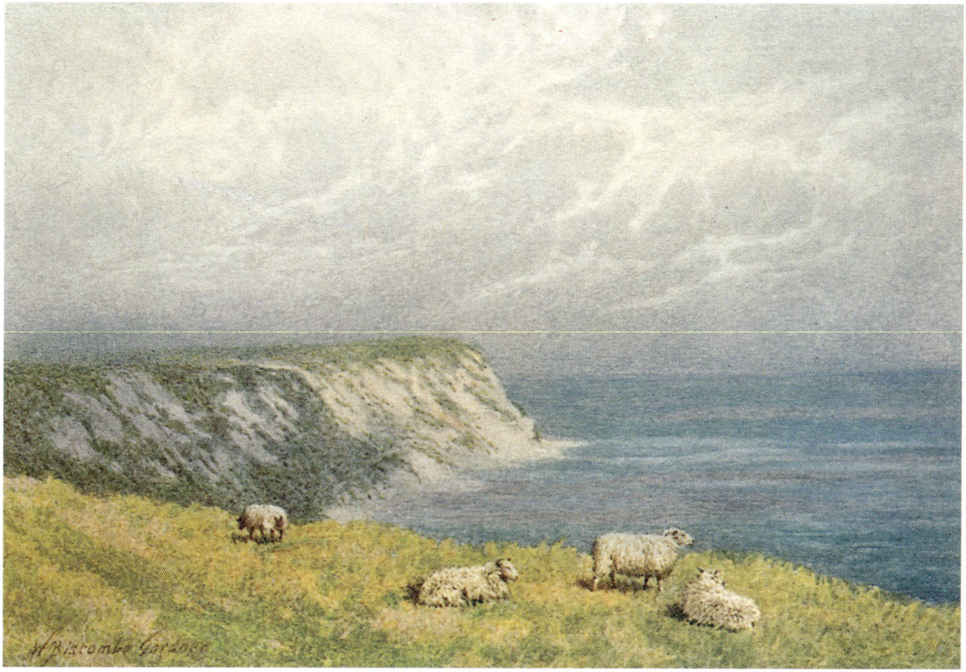

ABBOT'S CLIFF ABOVE THE WARREN, FOLKESTONE

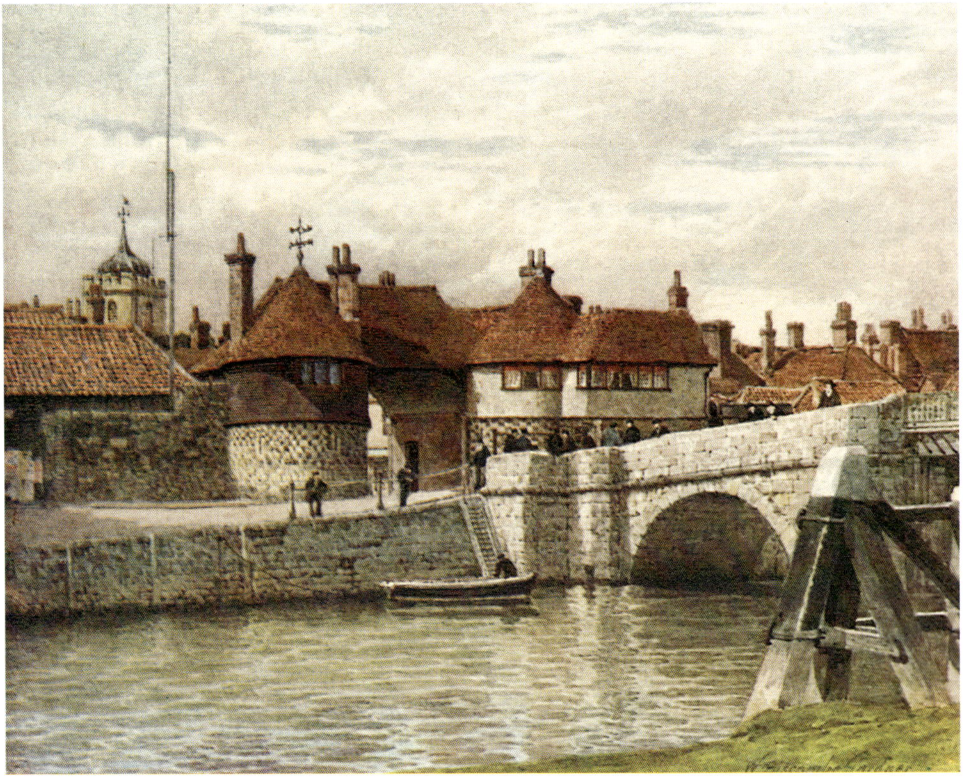

THE BARBICAN, SANDWICH